GRAND HOTELS: REFLECTIONS ON TIMELESS ARCHITECTURAL TREASURES

BY

Lynton Globa Viñas

Grand Hotels: Reflections on Timeless Architectural Treasures

TO:
My dear father, a man of honour who has always stood by me and accepted me the way I am and to my mentor, J. Wayne Frye.
…………Lynton Globa Viñas

And to the wonderful teachers, administrators and staff of the International Hotel School in Cape Town, South Africa. They offered me more than knowledge. They gave me friendship.
………..Lynton Globa Viñas

Copyright 2017 by Lynton Globa Viñas

All rights reserved. No part of this book or covers may be reproduced or transmitted in any form or by any other means, electronic or mechanical, including photocopying, recording, or by any information storage and retrieval system, without permission from the authors.

Catalogue Number: 2017-2453599

An Education Research Associates Publication
ISBN: 978-1-928183-27-3
Distributed by

Fireside Books – Victoria, British Columbia
Part of the Peninsula Publishing Consortium

Grand Hotels: Reflections on Timeless Architectural Treasures

TABLE OF CONTENTS

Prologue 1…..Page 5

Lynton Viñas and the Grand Adventure

Prologue 2 – Page 7

The Power of a Vision

Chapter 1 – Page 11

African Visions of Grandeur

Chapter 2 -41

European Architecture of Permanence

Chapter 3 - 91

Mid-Asian Reflections in a Golden Eye

Chapter 4 – 97

The Inscrutable East Asian Hotel Mystique

Chapter 5 - 111

South American Splendour

Chapter 6 - 119

Grand Hotels in the Land of Guns, Flags and Patriotism

Chapter 7 - 139

Oh Canada – Hotels in the Mists of Time

Epilogue - 165

A Vision into Reality

Grand Hotels: Reflections on Timeless Architectural Treasures

ABOUT THE AUTHOR

Lynton Viñas has been a manager and marketing guru for spas and beauty facilities, having worked her way up through the ranks. She is an accomplished singer and dancer who has performed at a variety of venues, and studied hotel management at the renowned International Hotel School in Cape Town, South Africa. She is from Laguna, Philippines and is a proud Canadian who lives on Vancouver Island in British Columbia.

She has worked at the famous African Pride Hotel at 15th on Orange in Cape Town, South Africa, the fantastic Protea Fire and Ice Hotel and the luxurious Mandela-Rhodes Suites Hotel. She is the author of many articles on management in the spa and hotel industry as well as the book about ghostly apparitions in hotels, *Haunted Hotels: Transitory Dances with the Dead*. Additionally, she is featured as the main character in the Lynton adolescent book series by Canadian author J. Wayne Frye.

She is also the author of *Astonishingly Remarkable and Unusual Hotels* and *A Concise Guide to Managing a Restaurant*.

Grand Hotels: Reflections on Timeless Architectural Treasures

PROLOGUE - PART 1
Lynton Viñas and the Grand Adventure

My primary function in this endeavour was to conduct extensive research and lay the foundations for a project that I was totally devoted to because of my intense interest in the hotel industry and how it has evolved over the years. Many years ago, giant chains did not dominate the industry, but rather, individually owned hotels were the norm, and they were lovingly handed down from one generation to the other with meticulous devotion to maintaining the high standards of service that made each individual hotel unique. This is not intended as an indictment of modern chains, because as part of my studies in hotel management I had the pleasure of working in a variety of capacities at the *African Pride Hotel*, which is a part of the over 6,000 hotels Marriott chain. Their devotion to service is second to none, and the way employees are treated is a profound testament to possibilities inherent in an organization that values those who often toil in obscurity unrecognized and unappreciated. The same can be said of the other hotels where I have worked in Cape Town: *Protea Fire and Ice* and *Mandela–Rhodes Suites Hotel*.

Unfortunately, only a small percentage of people can afford to stay or to dine at the world's most luxurious hotels. This is the way of a world where far too much of the good things only flow to those at the top of the economic ladder; however, it is that very opulent living that affords many people a livelihood serving those who can afford to stay at luxury hotels. I can truthfully say that in my experience working at hotels, no matter how affluent any of the guests might have been, they afforded the staff the utmost respect and were always appreciative of our efforts to make sure they had a grand experience. Don't misunderstand me, I am sure there are many rich people who are less than stellar in their behaviour towards those of us who are less affluent, but in my experience at the aforementioned five star hotels, I never encountered any extreme arrogance from the affluent guests.

I am a wordsmith who is prone to sometimes use extreme hyperbole in writing, so be warned that often words will flow in a cascade of colourful descriptions like water pouring over Niagara Falls. However, I hope you will be drenched with the excitement of a grand adventure!

PROLOGUE - PART 2
The Power of a Vision

In a world where the mundane mutterings of fools are reported as news, celebrities are aggrandized for extravagant lifestyles that are about as meaningful as a windshield wiper in a meteor shower, modern television entertainment is so banal that laugh tracks have to be inserted to cue us when to laugh and Jesus observing cow dung is considered art, it is comforting to know that architectural structures that can still truly titillate the senses with awe were once erected by magnificent artists who understood the true meaning of beauty.

It is said that beauty is often in the eye of the beholder. The most beautiful people I have encountered are those who have known defeat, known suffering, known struggle, known loss, and have found their way out of the depths. These persons have an appreciation, a sensitivity, and an understanding of life that fills them with compassion, gentleness and a deep loving concern. Truly beautiful people do not just happen; they are made with the pain and agony of this thing called life. Great architectural feats that titillate the senses were born of intense commitment to create beauty in a structure. It is not an accident that we can look at a grand structure like a hotel and realize that it is, in and of itself, a work of art. We can gaze at it as we would the *Mona Lisa* and appreciate the artist who brought a vision to life.

I often look at the modern world with disdain as I reflect on a time when television actually had opera, plays, symphonies and erudite discussions rather than *Dancing with the Stars* or a pack of rich malcontents (the *Kardashians,* for example*)* prancing around like peacocks. Stepping into a grand hotel from a by-gone era reminds me of just what man is capable of artistically achieving. These special hotels are not like most modern hotels that far too often seem transitory in nature and mirror man's existential predicament on earth. There is timeliness to these magnificent structures that transcends the mundane and lifts our spirits as we realize the grandeur of dreams that can be brought to reality.

History pays no heed to the unspectacular citizen who worked hard all day and walked at night to a humble home with sweat on the deep furrowed forehead that knows the pain of struggle. Many builders, too, knew the struggle for miracles in a world where their structures remain but they are forgotten. Architects with a vision are great warriors of grandeur in a world that often takes for granite their works of art.

Architecture from the gilded golden time when form reflected a sense of grandeur is the mirror of life from an age when man was still a free thinker and not married to the sameness that is modern society. The cookie cutter approach to everything from fast food to housing makes for a society that has today embraced the mundane and the usual as a way to make us all robotic servers in a banquet of banality. However, looking at the gloriously grand hotels of bygone days lets you feel the presence of the past, the spirit of a place, a reflection of the grandeur of a visionary time when everything did not revolve around servitude to the corporations that now control every walk of our lives to the point that we all are but mere oil in the machinery of capitalism that is grinding us up day by day in a world where the only thing that matters is the bottom line. Contemporary architects tend to impose modernity and sameness on everything. There may be a certain concern for history but it is not very deep. I understand that times have changed; we have evolved. But I do long for a time when the grandeur of human possibility soared like an ancient phoenix into the skies of hope. Architecture has to have roots, not be like the cottonwood tree that has roots so shallow that it tumbles over in a slight wind. Architecture should be like the mighty oak with a deep root system to make it endure!

Grand Hotels: Reflections on Timeless Architectural Treasures

A building should speak with the voice of majesty. It should resonate with depth and character. Visible from afar and unfailingly spectacular, buildings should be monuments, ideological markers endowed with an almost mystical aura by their positioning in space and expressive power. "By its incongruity, by its inhuman stature" writes the philosopher Jacques Derrida, "the monumental dimension serves to emphasize the non-representative nature of the very concept that it evokes." And what is the concept – it is the might and power of man's (or woman's) vision of beauty that is imagined and brought to life in a structure. So, let us take a journey into the world of architectural brilliance where dreams are reflected in structures that dance in the eyes which behold man's dreams of splendour at a time when creativity was not hemmed in by economic concerns, but rather, artistic embellishments were the norm not the exception. ……………Lynton Viñas

Grand Hotels: Reflections on Timeless Architectural Treasures

CHAPTER 1
African Visions of Grandeur

No list of iconic hotels can ever be complete in scope, so what I offer is highly subjective. These are the hotels I may have personally seen in many cases, even taking my own photographs. In a few instances, but rare, I have even been able to afford an overnight stay. Of course, many of the hotels I cover are ones that have been praised and glorified by friends, acquaintances, colleagues and accommodations aficionados over the years. As one might expect, there is particular glory in the European entries since it seems that is where some of the world's finest architecture glorifies a past when structures were built to last, not become instant tear-downs as is the norm for today's plastic-throw-away society. However, since the author has lived in Cape Town, South Africa during university attendance, I would like to start with African hotels. It is well known that one of the most famous places in Africa actually never existed. It is the iconic Rick's Café Americain from the movie, *Casablanca*. O.K., I grant that this is a book about famous hotels, but it is a rare grand hotel that does not have a restaurant. I must admit to spending many leisurely hours sipping tea or a diet coke at the namesake of this movie while reviewing plans for this book. Rick's Café Americain was only two blocks from my condo in the beautiful Gardens District of Cape Town. Could not my beloved other half help but imagine, as he sat sipping Diet Coke with me on the outdoor portion of the café, what it would have been like to be Bogart sitting iconically in the magnificent Rick's Café Americain in exotic Casablanca? And I could be Ingrid Bergman.

*Interior of Cape Town's
Iconic Rick's Café Americain,
where the spirit of Bogart lives.*

Grand Hotels: Reflections on Timeless Architectural Treasures

*Lounge area at the renowned Rick's Café Americain.
Unfortunately, there is no piano player there named Sam.*

1. The Mount Nelson Hotel – Cape Town, South Africa

Only about two hundred metres from Rick's Café Americain is the magnificent Mount Nelson Hotel, with soaring entry columns that are a prelude to the amplitude that waits down the brick roadway. Shipping magnate Sir Donald Currie, who envisioned an

Grand Hotels: Reflections on Timeless Architectural Treasures

edifice that would rival any hotel in London at the time, completed the hotel a scant eight months before the beginning of the Boar War. British war lords, General Sir Redvers Buller, Lord Kitchener and Lord Roberts, were frequent guests.

Rudyard Kipling called it a rival to the Taj Mahal, and it is rumoured that Winston Churchill formulated plans here with the aforementioned war lords for concentration camps to house the Boar women and children who were rounded up in masse. Of the 107,000 people interned in the camps, 27,927 Boers died, along with an unknown number of black Africans. It was this method, along with the U.S.A.'s reservation system for Native Americans that was the prototype for Hitler's concentration camps for Jews, Gypsies and homosexuals.

Although the belief in racial superiority was a mainstay in South Africa from its inception, it was home for two of history's greatest humanitarians who fought against racism, Mohandas Ghandi and Nelson Mandela. The purpose of this book is to revel in the grandeur of magnificent hotels, not explore politics, but no structures can ever be totally separated from the conditions that existed at the time in which they were built. For example, most of the labour for this hotel, including many of the highly skilled artisans, were black South Africans who toiled in obscurity to, as is also common today, build a structure for the privileged to stay in while those who did the really hard work constructing it could not afford to spend a night in these grand edifices.

Grand Hotels: Reflections on Timeless Architectural Treasures

Afternoon tea at the "Nellie" is on the bucket list of many intrepid world travellers, as is seeing the old clock in the lobby which was famous for being so loud it could be heard by ships docking in Cape Town Waterfront. Today, it has been repaired to emit softer chimes.

The hotel, it seems, has been on a near-constant expansion programme since its inception. Historic buildings and sets of new rooms have been added to the hotel complex, as was the first heated swimming pool in Africa. And of course, it is also a favourite haunt of the rich and famous, so if you can afford a stay, no telling who might pop into the bar.

With Table Mountain nearby, the views are breathtaking.

The following is a short history of the hotel:

- 1899: Mount Nelson was the first hotel in South Africa to offer hot and cold running water. It was described as being "even better than its London counterparts." Its first advertisement in the *Cape Times* newspaper, 3 March 1899 read: "This large and splendid hotel, beautifully situated in the Gardens at the Top of Government Avenue, in the most Airy and Healthy part of Cape Town, offers to Visitors all the comforts of a First-class Hotel at Reasonable Charges."
- 1899: The South African Second Boer War began in October. The British used Mount Nelson Hotel as a headquarters from which to plan their military campaign.
- 1919: Cape Town was ravaged by a deadly influenza virus. The city's medical doctors designated Mount Nelson Hotel a "plague-free zone."
- 1925: The Prince of Wales visited the hotel (the "Prince of Wales Gate" and palm-lined driveway were built in honour of this visit). Sir Arthur Conan Doyle (the creator of Sherlock Holmes) stayed at the hotel later that year.
- 1973: The Oasis accommodation wing was added to Mount Nelson Hotel's main house and new restaurants and spas were opened.
- 1988: Mount Nelson Hotel was purchased by Orient-Express Hotels.

Grand Hotels: Reflections on Timeless Architectural Treasures

- 1990: A row of eight perfectly restored historic cottages on the hotel grounds were converted into the Garden Cottage Suites.
- 1993: An electrical fire caused extensive damage to the hotel, resulting in it having to be closed for six months.
- 1996: Mount Nelson Hotel acquired three historic buildings adjacent to Palm Avenue, and Helmsley Hotel, and all four buildings were restored and converted into guest accommodations. Taunton House Cottage was originally built as a guesthouse, Green Park was originally a hostel for nursing staff, and Hof Villa was built as a private residence for the hotel manager. The Helmsley was originally the site of the first Jewish service in Cape Town (held in 1841) and thereafter it became the first Hebrew Congregation in South Africa.
- 2014: Orient-Express Hotels changed its name to Belmond Ltd. and hotel was renamed Belmond Mount Nelson Hotel.

Views from all 220 rooms are spectacular!

Grand Hotels: Reflections on Timeless Architectural Treasures

The famous who have bedded down here include: Agatha Christie, Marlene Dietrich, Robert Wagner, Shirley Bassey, Henry Kissinger, Donald Sutherland, Al Gore, Liberace, Nicholas Cage, Hillary Swank, Phil Collins, Ethan Hawke, David Bowie and Iman, Janet Jackson, Margaret Thatcher, George Bush I, U-2 and Bono, Jane Seymour, M. Night Shayamalan, Billy Joel, John Malkovich, Paris Hilton, Nelson Mandela, Charlize Theron, Opray Winfrey, Colin Farrell, the Dali Lama, Leonardo Di Caprio, Richard Gere, Michael Buble, Robin Williams and Morgan Freedom.

This hotel is listed as one of the best places in the world for afternoon tea. The elegant dining room brings a special charm as you sip tea and munch on biscuits.

Grand Hotels: Reflections on Timeless Architectural Treasures

It is said that a truly great hotel has a feeling, a dynamic that sets it apart. If you enter the facility from Orange Street, with its massive arch and stately columns, you are overwhelmed with anticipation for what is down the brick road.

A twilight stroll is peaceful and relaxing as the setting sun twinkles and dances off the glistening pink facades.

No two rooms are alike, and each one is finished with intensive devotion to detail that accentuates luxury.

Grand Hotels: Reflections on Timeless Architectural Treasures

The hotel's design was heavily influenced by Daniel Currie himself, who hired the London architectural firm of Dunn and Watson that insisted the builder be William Cubitt and Company, also of London. The attention to detail demanded by Currie often perplexed Mr. Dunn, who proclaimed the hotel one of his most frustrating endeavours.

Main entry to the hotel on Orange Street in Cape Town.

2. Granddaddy Hotel – Cape Town

It is logical to assume that iconic hotels come with a high price tag, but that is not necessarily the case with the Granddaddy. Situated on vibrant, delightful Long Street in City Centre, the

Grand Hotels: Reflections on Timeless Architectural Treasures

street itself is famous as a bohemian hangout and is lined with book stores, various ethnic restaurants and bars. Long Street exhibits a diversified culture and attracts tourists from all over the world. Several theatres which showed anti-apartheid plays were located on the street during the 1970s and 1980s, although all have now closed and been replaced by trendy restaurants or stores. Architecturally it is noted for its Victorian buildings with wrought iron balconies.

Can a street be alive? Just ask anyone who has strolled Bourbon Street in New Orleans that question. Long Street is the Bourbon Street of Cape Town, without the giddiness and garishness. There are no strip joints, no street vendors hawking alcoholic drinks, but there is an innate liveliness, a pulsating rhythm that moans like old Louie Satchmo Armstrong wailing on his trumpet or Pete Fountain making his clarinet moan with the sounds of love lost and love found. This street sways with the vibrancy of the new South Africa; a multi-racial, multi-ethnic, open-minded society that embraces humanity in all its glory, and right smack-dab in the middle of all this is the majestic Granddaddy that has a unique beat of its own. It is a Mother City original that bustles with an energy that is uniquely Cape Town.

Originally named the Metropole, it took on a new name when it was sold in 2008. Fortunately, its charm was not renovated but enhanced. Although this hotel has been refurbished and altered a number of times in more than a century, the basic design remains much as it was when it opened in 1895 as Hotel Metropole. Today, as in yesterday, it is imposing and grand in appearance, being designed in the old German Renaissance style. The original construction was from a plan by the Dutch architect, Anthony De Witt, who came to South Africa in 1879. William Black, an Australian architect, undertook renovations in 1900. Although it is small, it offers the visitor a grandeur that is often reserved for more imposing structures.

The Granddaddy stands majestic and proud on Long Street.

It is often said that a hotel's uniqueness starts from the bottom up, but this is a place where the top down approach says volumes about the unusual nature of this magnificent structure. After all, there is nothing ordinary about a rooftop trailer park in the centre of the city. Yes, I said a trailer park! There are seven Streamline Trailers on the roof of this iconic hotel.

Seven authentic Air Stream Trailers have their own décor theme and offer the opportunity to take in breathtaking views of the city and Table Mountain.

Grand Hotels: Reflections on Timeless Architectural Treasures

1950's style décor is used in the trailers and rooms.

Also on the rooftop is an open air cinema – public welcome.

Grand Hotels: Reflections on Timeless Architectural Treasures

Although one is impressed with what is on top, what is below is equally impressive, with attention to detail that reflects a commitment to maintain old world charm with modern amenities that make a stay here a truly exciting experience that titillates the senses.

The Granddaddy Restaurants

Grand Hotels: Reflections on Timeless Architectural Treasures

Each room is decorated differently with an intense eye to detail and a commitment to a welcoming, relaxing atmosphere.

We live in a chaotic world where the mundane is passed off as the norm, but there is nothing mundane about the Granddaddy. The deep hues on the floors and the intricately polished walls glisten and dance with the ambiance of 1950's peacefulness and serenity. Although the times are probably overly romanticized, as one sips a drink on the rooftop bar among the Streamline trailers, there is a sense that you are part of a time when things were simpler and the world was a more tranquil place.

3. Lanzerac Wine Estate Hotel – Stellenbosch, South Africa

Although not always a hotel, this estate has been around since 1692. Home to the first bottled Pinotage, it is situated at the foot of the majestic Jonkershoek Mountain.

If you love wine, this is a holiday made in heaven, since this estate produces some of the finest wines in the world, and tasting is part of the accommodation package.

Grand Hotels: Reflections on Timeless Architectural Treasures

Isaac Shrijver was the Indiana Jones of his time. When he was not going into the uncharted wilds in search of treasure, he was embarking on trading trips into the Great Karoo Area, climbing towering mountains or chasing the pot of gold at the end of a rainbow. Lanzerac's history dates back to 1692 when Governer Simon van der Stel granted a considerable tract of land in the Jonkershoek Valley to Isaac Schrijver and three freed slaves who set about planting vineyards. Throughout the years, the farm had many owners. The most notable being Mrs. Elizabeth Katherina English, who purchased the farm in 1914, then called Schoongezicht. She changed the name of the farm to Lanzerac.

1925 saw the birth here of South Africa's first, unique and indigenous wine grape variety Pinotage, which was a cross between Pinot Noir and Hermitage.

In 1958 a young man named David Rawdon bought Lanzerac and spent a year renovating the property into a world-class country hotel. Rawdon searched for neglected pieces of antique furniture and brought them to Lanzerac. Long lists of famous people have spent time here, including British royals, famous comedians and American politicians - some also comedians.

The modern-day Lanzerac Hotel & Spa still retains its old Cape Dutch charm, offering world travellers a choice of 48 luxury rooms, complete with views of vineyards and the sweep of the nearby Helderberg Mountains.

Grand Hotels: Reflections on Timeless Architectural Treasures

Luxury accommodations with bathrooms that rival those anywhere in the world for lavishness makes guests feel like royalty.

Grand Hotels: Reflections on Timeless Architectural Treasures

There is an old world ambiance at Lanzerac.

4. Grogan's Castle Hotel – Tsavo Plains, Kenya

Alright, this is a favourite of author Wayne Frye, because he once wrote a short story about man-eating lions in Tsavo. The story was based on the true adventure of John Henry Patterson, who went from England to the Tsavo area to build the East African rail line between Kenya and Uganda. Some readers may have seen the movie (*The Ghost and the Darkness* staring Michael Douglas and Val Kilmer) about this true story of two lions that may have killed as many as 100 railroad workers before Patterson managed to kill them. The stuffed remains of the two man-eaters are on display at Chicago's Field Museum of Natural History. For a point of reference, the term Tsavo means "place of slaughter" in the Kamba language. However, there are no man-eaters left in the area, so the guests who stay at Grogan's Castle Hotel should have no fear of any lion attacks.

Grand Hotels: Reflections on Timeless Architectural Treasures

The quiet at this magnificent hotel can sometimes be deafening. There is nothing but open plains for 12 kilometres, where the small town of Taveta is located. However, in the distance, one can see the towering Mount Kilimanjaro.

There is a serene magical quality to the place as one drives up the hillside. All around are rolling plains with the mighty Kilimanjaro rising majestically in the distance.

Grogan's Castle was started in 1930 by Ewart Grogan, who was an adventurer possessed of magnetic charm, a formidable intellect and a near boundless ego. He finished Grogan's Castle in the mid 1930's and lived there until the late 1950's. He commenced a grand expedition from Cape Town to Cairo at the age of 24, reaching Cairo in 1900, after two and a half years of traveling. He had been stalked by lions, hippos and crocodiles, pursued by head-hunters and cannibals, plagued by parasites and fevers. Thus, he was dubbed the "Great Grogan," and he loved the name. He was indeed the first man to traverse Africa from south to north.

Kilimanjaro, with snow at its summit is a stark contrast to the rolling, hot plains of Tsavo below. Of course, global warming has led to much less snow today. Yet, the words of renowned author, Ernest Hemingway, in his short story, The Snows of Kilimanjaro, are still apropos: "Its western summit is called the Masai 'Ngaje Ngai', the House of God."

Grand Hotels: Reflections on Timeless Architectural Treasures

The sparsely furnished entryway reflects the nature of the plains of Tsavo. However, you step up, and like gazing at Kilimanjaro, you are awed by what you see.

Although out of the way for most travellers, this is a hotel with character that sets it apart from many other iconic hotels, simply because of its unusual location in the Tsavo National Park. The grassy plains of Tsavo stretch as far as the eye can see, meeting the clear blue skies on the horizon with the mighty Kilimanjaro in the distance. In the midst of this magnificence, like a giant beacon shining its light of beauty, rises a hillside castle that titillates the eyes and assaults the senses. You have arrived in a paradise on the plains of time.

5. Victoria Falls Hotel – Victoria Falls, Zimbabwe

The Cairo to Cape Town Rail Road Line was an inducement that led to the erection of the Victoria Falls Hotel in 1904. With dramatic views of the gorges of Victoria Falls, the hotel offers magnificent vistas of the gorges and bridge from many rooms.

The history of The Victoria Falls Hotel is incomplete without reference to the development of the railway system in Zimbabwe. Cecil Rhodes (Rhodes' Scholarships) and Charles Metcalfe built a railroad bridge across the Zambezi River, insisting that the spray from the falls should splash the train which is why the site was chosen in close proximity to the falls. The Victoria Falls Hotel was built and operated by the railways administration, but in the early 1970s it was leased to African Sun Hotels Limited. Today the property itself still belongs to the National Railways of Zimbabwe and there is a shared 50/50 partnership operation between African Sun and Zimbabwe.

Grand Hotels: Reflections on Timeless Architectural Treasures

It has been called by John Creewl in his book *100 Years of the Victoria Falls Hotel* one of the truly special places in the world. He notes that the most important factor behind the hotel's success has been its close proximity to one of the most remarkable sights in the world – Victoria Falls. This hotel serves as a stark reminder of the distinguished and elegant era in which it was built, a time when the grandiose was the norm in a world that embraced quality and people took great pride in their workmanship.

The hotel lies within a vast manicured garden which has an unobstructed view of the Victoria Falls Bridge and the spray of the falls can be felt on your face. A private path leads guests from the gardens to the entrance of the Victoria Falls rainforest which surrounds the hotel. And, of course, the roar of the falls can be heard in all its glory, making one feel in complete awe of its power.

The corridors of the hotel reflect the historical link to the era in which it was created with drawings, paintings and photographs of the major political figures of the day adorning the elaborately carved walls. Each step reminds the guest of the incredible dedication it took to bring this place to life. There is a feeling that seems to creep into the veins, making the blood flow faster and the breathing become shallow as you realize that this is not just a hotel, but a path to embracing a time and era when life was simpler and structures were a work of art.

Grand Hotels: Reflections on Timeless Architectural Treasures

There is a grand expansive that embraces the great outdoors.
Soothing piano melodies add to the dining experience.

Grand Hotels: Reflections on Timeless Architectural Treasures

View from some of the rooms.

Grand Hotels: Reflections on Timeless Architectural Treasures

There are few sights as overwhelming as Victoria Falls, and this magnificent hotel puts it at your feet. Called by one tribe "the smoke that thunders," it is the only waterfall in the world with a length of more than a kilometre and a height of more than one hundred meters. It is considered to be the largest fall in the world.

The Victoria Falls Hotel is a grand lady of the Edwardian-era, which has private footpaths that all lead to one of the Seven Natural Wonders of the World. The hotel is surrounded by carefully tended tropical gardens, lily ponds and centuries-old shade trees. Of course, the fantastic panoramas figure prominently during afternoon tea, which is served on Stanley Terrace, overlooking the Victoria Falls Bridge that links Zimbabwe to Zambia.

Grand Hotels: Reflections on Timeless Architectural Treasures

CHAPTER 2

European Architecture of Permanence

Where else but Europe can one sleep in a luxurious palace, watch waves pound the rocks around an ancient lighthouse that is now a hotel, feel like a knight as you settle into your room in a castle, or cuddle up with a good book as you listen for ghosts in the corridors of a chateau. These are the remnants of a time when empires were built and European culture refined. The architects who crafted these magnificent structures have faded into history, but their monuments to another time still stand as glorious reminders that mankind was capable of great feats of beauty crafted by skilled artisans who were masters of their crafts and took great pride in their work. Authentic heritage, combined with high standards of service and the finest gastronomic experiences, titillate the senses and embrace human appreciation for palaces of pleasure that are harmonious testaments to visionary artists who saw beauty in a structure. It has been said that no stream rises higher than its source. What ever man might build could never express or reflect more than he was. He could record neither more nor less than he had learned of life when the buildings were built, and that life in Europe produced some of the most enduring structures ever erected.

War entails human suffering, and so it is with buildings. Normalities of form are often shattered and conventions tossed aside as architects, craftsmen and labourers join forces, fighting a war against the mundane to erect monuments to their visions. It can often be a lonely battle as outside forces and pressures abound to sully perfection. Michelangelo suffered blindness from paint dripping into his eyes as he painted the murals on the ceilings of the Sistine Chapel, but he never wavered in his devotion to his art. Every artist dips his brush in his own soul, and paints his own nature into his or her artistic endeavour. Architects are artists and their canvases are the buildings they design. In Europe, these master builders have left a lasting testament to their artistic integrity, and we shall now look at examples of how they have left their souls in places of grandeur that are their masterpieces. When I say artist, I mean the person who is building things, creatively moulding a vision, whether it be pottery from a kiln, minerals mined to create jewels, a haunting image on canvas or a building soaring skyward to proclaim man's enduring nature. It is all a big game of construction, and some work with a brushes, some with shovels, some with mortar and bricks, some with words as done here.

Picasso said, "The artist is a receptacle for emotions that come from all over the place: from the sky, from the earth, from a scrap of paper, from a passing shape, from a spider's web."

6. Dolder Grand Hotel - Zurich, Switzerland

Between 1897 and 1899, the Dolder Grand Hotel & Curhaus was built under the direction of architect Jacques Gros as a place of relaxation and regeneration for people in need of a rest. At first it was open only in the summers due to heavy snowfall in winters around the area. Today, it spreads out over 40,000 square metres and is connected to nearby Zurich by a highway and a direct rail line.

Every year, for culinary connoisseurs, the hotel has a four day feast, inviting famous chefs from all over the world to practice their skills, serving up delightful concoctions to those who appreciate fine dining. If you are planning to munch on these culinary masterpieces, the waiting list is rather long, so you will have time to develop a voracious appetite.

On a hillside and only a 15-minute funicular and tram journey from central Zurich, the Dolder brands itself as a city resort and has an impressive roster of facilities to back up the claim, including a golf course, a 4,000 square metre spa and an ice rink that opens on the grounds each winter.

Grand Hotels: Reflections on Timeless Architectural Treasures

Yesterday

Today

Grand Hotels: Reflections on Timeless Architectural Treasures

Lynton Globa Viñas

Grand Hotels: Reflections on Timeless Architectural Treasures

Those who enjoy lavish accommodations with big spaces will feel right at home here.

7. Dromoland Castle Hotel & Country Estate
Newmarket-on-Fergus, Ireland

"The main hallway of the Sternwood place was two stories high. Over the entrance doors, which would have let in a troop of Indian elephants, there was a broad stained-glass panel showing a knight in dark armour rescuing a lady who was tied to a tree and didn't have any clothes on but some very long and convenient hair. The knight had pushed the visor of his helmet back to be sociable, and he was fiddling with the knots on the ropes that tied the lady to the tree and not getting anywhere. I stood there and thought that if I lived in the house, I would sooner or later have to climb up there and help him. He didn't seem to be really trying." — Raymond Chandler, The Big Sleep

Chandler would have loved Dromoland Castle, because it is all he described above and much more. Even Bogart, as Sam Spade, would have loved this place. Unfortunately, there are no nude damsels in distress for noble knights of the day to rescue and ride off with on trusty steeds to a serene nearby waterfall for a romantic interlude. However, there is a grand countryside with unimaginable beauty and a hotel that bristles with the delight of a bygone era that is, no doubt, overly romanticized, but what is wrong with a little fanciful daydreaming in a magical kingdom called Ireland. Knighthood lives in the hearts and minds of those of us forever trapped in our youth. It rises above eternity and lets us all be dragon slayers.

Grand Hotels: Reflections on Timeless Architectural Treasures

*This is more than a hotel – it is an adventure
on the plains of time where one can feel
the way things must have been "back in the day."*

Dromoland Castle is built entirely of dark blue limestone with detailed workmanship. The ornamental grounds and woods extend over more than 1,500 acres. Dromoland is one of the most famous baronial castles in Ireland and was the ancestral home of the O'Brien's, Barons of Inchiquin, who are one of the few native Gaelic families of royal blood and direct descendants of Brian Boroimhe (Boru), High King of Ireland in the eleventh century. A brief history is below:

1002-1014

Brian Boru ruled Ireland as High King from his throne in Killaloe.

1014

Donough O'Brien, a son of Brian Boru, controlled Dromoland when it was a defensive stronghold. For the next 900 years a branch of the O'Briens lived at Dromoland Castle.

1543

The chief of the Clan O'Brien, Murrough, 57th King of Thomond was forced to surrender his royalty to King Henry VII, thus becoming the Baron of Inchiquin and First Earl of Thomond.

1651

Conor O'Brien of Lemenagh Castle was killed in battle. His widow, Maire, agreed to marry an officer in the Cromwellian army in order to save the family estate. She married John Cooper, thus preserving the estate for her dear eldest son, Sir Donough O'Brien.

1660

Sir Donough O'Brien moved the most powerful branch of the Obrien's to Dromoland in the late 17th century. He was an astute man and managed to avoid declaring for either King James II or King William. He was at that time reputed to be the richest man in Ireland.

1730

Sir Edward O'Brien was revered as a famous racehorse owner and trainer. He built the Turret on the hill opposite the entrance to Dromoland Estate, from where he would observe his horses race. He once gambled the estate on a horse race; mercifully, he won the race.

1700-1730

When the second castle/house at Dromoland was built; it was more residential in appearance with a design of the Queen Anne period. The Queen Anne Court, the charming quadrangle of 29 guestrooms, is a century older than the rest of today's castle. It was remodelled inside and redecorated in 1963 when the castle was redesigned as a hotel.

1800-1836

The present main building of Dromoland Castle, with its high Gothic-styled grey stone walls, was rebuilt and designed by the Pain brothers, famous architects of that period. The castle was built by the then Lord of Dromoland, Sir Edward O'Brien, 4th Baronet, at great expense.

Grand Hotels: Reflections on Timeless Architectural Treasures

1803-1864

Dromoland Castle was the birthplace and boyhood home of William Smith O'Brien, Member of Parliament. Despite his aristocratic background, Smith O'Brien fought militantly for the rights of oppressed Irish Catholic peasant farmers and led the Young Irelanders' Rebellion against the British authorities in 1848. He was sentenced to be hanged, drawn and quartered, later exiled instead to Tasmania for his role in the revolt. He returned to Ireland in 1856. There is a statue of him in O'Connell Street, Dublin. He died in 1864.

1880-1921

The wealth of the Barons of Inchiquin dwindled after a series of Land Acts started in the 1880s. During this time, landlords were compelled to sell their tenanted farmlands, thus the Inchiquins lost their main source of income. They still considered themselves fortunate, as their castle had survived the troubled times of Ireland's revolutionary war against Britain. The homes of many landlords in Ireland were left in ruins during the Irish Republican Army's war against the British forces in 1920 and 1921.

1921-1922

The Irish Republican Army leaders in Dublin marked Dromoland Castle for destruction. However, sabotage orders were reversed at the last minute at the urgent request of local IRA leaders in County Clare, who argued that the Inchiquin Lords had been fair and benevolent in dealing with their tenant farmers. Sir Lucius O'Brien, the 13th Baron of Inchiquin (brother of Sir William Smith O'Brien), was remembered respectfully by the people of County Clare for his relief work in the famine years of the 1840s.

1922-1940

Although the family's good reputation saved the castle during the revolution, the later loss of income after the forced sale of the tenant farms made the castle and the 2,000 acre estate increasingly difficult for the Inchiquins to keep. After the death of the 15th Baron of Inchiquin in 1929, Dromoland was supported mainly by the personal wealth of his widow, Lady Ethel Inchiquin, an heiress, whose portrait, painted by Herbert Draper, hangs near the staircase in the castle's hall.

1940-1962

After Lady Ethel's death, her oldest son, Sir Donough O'Brien, the 16th Baron of Inchiquin, and his wife, Lady Anne, daughter of Viscount Chelmsford, a Viceroy of India, managed to maintain Dromoland Castle as a traditional ancestral home for more than twenty years. Lord Inchiquin tried to make the estate self-supporting as a dairy farm, but by 1948 was so financially hard pressed that he began to take in tourists as paying guests.

1962-1986

Lord Inchiquin sold the castle, along with some 330 acres of surrounding land, and the hunting and fishing rights to Mr.

Bernard McDonough, an American industrialist, whose grandparents were born in Ireland. Conor O'Brien, the 18th baron, and his family live in Thomond House and continue to farm and run part of the ancestral homeland as a sporting and leisure estate.

The castle underwent major renovations to transform the ancestral home into a luxury hotel. When the castle was officially reopened as a Resort Hotel, visitors who remembered it from the days of the Inchiquins marvelled at the preservation of its stately, warm and cheerful baronial country house atmosphere. The public rooms on the main floor of the castle look very much the same now as when Lord Inchiquin's family lived there, although the Lord's octagonal shaped study, under the round tower, is now a pleasant cocktail bar, and his library is now part of the dining room.

1987-Present

A consortium of mainly Irish American investors purchased the castle and estate. Through their continued investment and management, the castle has enjoyed a worldwide reputation for excellence and is regarded as one of the great resorts in Europe.

Grand Hotels: Reflections on Timeless Architectural Treasures

Grand Hotels: Reflections on Timeless Architectural Treasures

Tucked away in a tranquil, peaceful place that seems lost in time, one cannot but feel that there is something magical about this hotel. The sprawling grounds give one a feeling of floating endlessly in a sea of tranquility where time and space seem irrelevant and the outside world is so distant that nothing is able to penetrate the serenity and placidity of a land where you can feel the grandeur of a time when all seemed right in the world. Was that time illusionary at best? Of course it was, as most times are. It was romanticized and fictionalized, but why can we not be lost in illusions on occasion? We need a retreat from the modern world that too often overwhelms us. This magnificent retreat offers a grand illusion from that by-gone era that lets us forget for a day, a night or a week, the jungles of concrete and steel that are too often our personal prisons.

8. Hotel Sacher Wein – Vienna, Austria

This is not one of those out of the way hotels in the pristine countryside, but alas, this is Vienna – once home to Ludwig van Beethoven, Johannes Brahms and many other famous composers who needed the magic of Vienna for inspiration. Ah, and what of Mozart who journeyed from Salzburg to Vienna in 1781, and found acclaim. He said of Vienna: "I earn little money here, but I know fame, because the Viennese people appreciate my art."

Grand Hotels: Reflections on Timeless Architectural Treasures

The Hotel Sacher Wein is a five star monument to magnificence situated near the famed Vienna Opera House. Within its walls are some of the finest art works from the 19th century, but the hotel itself is also a work of art. Antonio Vivaldi called the hotel home for a large part of his life.

The hotel was founded in 1876 by Eduard Sacher. His father, a confectioner had become famous for his Sachertorte, which is stylized chocolate concoction still served in the restaurant today. In 1890, Eduard married a woman named Anna Fuchs who became hotel manager. She quickly earned a reputation for both her commercial skills and her eccentricity, never being seen without her trusty bulldogs and a cigar dangling from her lips. Under her reign, Hotel Sacher became one of the finest hotels in the world, where the aristocracy and diplomats congregated. However, after World War I, Anna's penchant for upholding the upper-class reputation of the hotel led to her denying service to guests of non-aristocratic descent, at the same time granting generous credit to impoverished aristocrats. Her management style caused financial problems and led to bankruptcy and change of ownership in 1934 when it was acquired by the Gürtler family and the building was extensively renovated. After the end of World War II, allied occupied Austria, like Germany, was divided into four zones by the victorious powers. Vienna, like Berlin, was also subdivided into four zones. During the occupation, the British used the hardly damaged hotel as their

Grand Hotels: Reflections on Timeless Architectural Treasures

headquarters and it appears prominently in Carol Reed's classic film staring Orson Welles and Joseph Cotton, *The Third Man*, as script writer Graham Greene was a regular at the hotel bar while doing research in Vienna. The famous guests include a long list of entertainers and politicians, the most prominent being John F. Kennedy, who is rumoured to have had a two day liaison with a famous actress at the hotel.

A night time arrival is recommended as the sight of the Hotel Sacher Wein after sunset is particularly gratifying.

Grand Hotels: Reflections on Timeless Architectural Treasures

Beautiful architecture yes, but just look at the beauty below!

Yes, this is the famous concoction of the elder Sache, and the recipe has not been altered after all these years.

Grand Hotels: Reflections on Timeless Architectural Treasures

Rooms are spacious and filled with antiques.

9. Four Seasons Hotel Gresham Palace – Budapest Hungary

This is another hotel I recommend for night arrival to enjoy the true scope of magnificence. The site of this incredible hotel was once occupied by Nákó House, a neo-classical palace built in 1827. In 1880, the London-based Gresham Life Assurance Company bought the property, at a time when it was illegal to invest money in stocks (image that – exerting some control over the insurance industry), but rental income was a wise investment.

Grand Hotels: Reflections on Timeless Architectural Treasures

The company later decided to build its foreign headquarters on the site, but wanted a more grandiose appearance. Architects Zsigmond Quittner and Jozsef Vago designed the new structure, and in 1904, they began construction of the Gresham Palace, which opened in 1907. It was named after the 16th century English financier Sir Thomas Gresham, the founder of the Royal Exchange in London.

During the occupation after World War II, the Red Army used the building as a barracks and over the years it fell into disrepair. When the communist era ended in 1990, the government, as was normal for most former communist regimes, began the gradual dismantling of state owned enterprises and the building was sold, like so many other things, to capitalists who embarked on renovations that offered the rich and privileged the very finest accommodations money could buy. Where the common people used to live in state provided apartments, today only the rich can afford the pleasure of this monument to excess in all its glory. Still, despite being an avowed socialist, the author of this book must humbly and graciously admit to bowing before the artistic endeavours of the capitalists who preserved this Art Nouveau masterpiece.

Overlooking a park on the banks of the Danube River, this lavish hotel is in the very heart of magical Budapest, and the great magician, Houdini, was born near here as were the three Gabor sisters (Zsa Zsa, Eva, Magda).

Grand Hotels: Reflections on Timeless Architectural Treasures

Inside and outside, this place makes a lasting impression.

Lynton Globa Viñas

Grand Hotels: Reflections on Timeless Architectural Treasures

Even taking a swim at the Gresham Palace is a surreal experience.

One of the restaurants has private cubicles for dining.
And it is rumoured one of the candelabras belonged to Liberace.

Grand Hotels: Reflections on Timeless Architectural Treasures

10. The Hotel Ritz – Paris

Grand Hotels: Reflections on Timeless Architectural Treasures

As a writer, this hotel has a special place in my heart, because it was Ernest Hemingway's favourite hangout before World War II. Hemingway was broke, but was given free drinks when he discovered the Ritz in the late 1920s in the company of fellow writer, Scott Fitzgerald. Together, the two men formulated ideas for some of the most iconic books ever written. However, Hemingway's most memorable sojourn at the Ritz was when he liberated the beloved hotel bar from the Germans in 1944. As told by *News France*, Hemingway's actions as the French capital was freed from its Nazi occupiers, is the stuff of legend. Hemingway, a war correspondent for the *American Collier's Magazine*, was embedded with the US 4th Division troops that landed on the Normandy beaches on June 6, 1944. Over the next two months he stuck with the foot soldiers as they marched towards Paris in support of the French 2nd Armoured Division, which entered the capital on August 25. It is said that Hemingway once intonated that his idea of heaven was sitting in the bar at the Ritz. One resistance fighter said, "Hemingway talked of nothing else but the liberation of the bar at the Ritz."

Hemingway managed, using his famous name and with the help of the American General, George Patton, to wrangle a meeting with French commander General Philippe Leclerc. His request was simple and compelling to a hard drinker like Hemingway. He simply wanted to be given enough men to go and liberate the Ritz's bar.

Grand Hotels: Reflections on Timeless Architectural Treasures

He got a frosty reception and was dismissed. However, Hemingway persevered and on August 25, dressed in his correspondent's military uniform, he arrived at the hotel in a commandeered jeep with a machine gun and a group of Resistance fighters. He burst into the hotel and announced that he had come to personally liberate it and its bar, which had been requisitioned in June 1940 by the Nazis and occupied by German dignitaries, including, on occasion, Hermann Goering and Joseph Goebbels. Hemingway approached the manager of the hotel, Claude Auzello, and asked: "Where are the Germans? I have come to liberate the Ritz."

"Monsieur," he replied, "They left a long time ago. And I can not let you enter with a weapon."

Hemingway walked outside, put the gun in the jeep and came back to the bar where he is said to have run up a tab for 50 dry Martinis. Hemingway searched the cellar with his men, taking two prisoners and finding an excellent stock of brandy, which he shared with the prisoners.

Inspecting the upper floors and roofs they found nothing, except for some sheets that the Germans had riddled with bullets. Hemingway wrote later that he could not stand the thought that the Germans had soiled the room he shared with Mary Welsh, whom he would marry in 1946.

One of the drunken prisoners is rumoured to have said, "If I'd know I'd be treated like this, I'd have surrendered long ago."

The Ritz's head barman said of Hemingway, "He wore the uniform and gave orders with such authority that many thought he was a general."

Today, there is a smaller bar in the hotel, fittingly called the Hemingway Bar.

Since the Ritz's opening in 1898, it has attracted people from all walks of life. Unfortunately, today, only the elite, because of the prices, can afford to stay here. It is ranked among the most luxurious hotels in the world. It was closed from 2011 until 2016 for remodelling at cost of 400 million U. S. dollars.

Grand Hotels: Reflections on Timeless Architectural Treasures

Now, there is an interesting story of chicanery and intrigue connected with how this hotel became known as the Ritz. The façade was designed by the royal architect Jules Mansart. In 1854, it was acquired by the Péreire brothers, who made it the head office of their financial institution. In 1888, the Swiss hotelier, César Ritz and the French chef, August Escoffier, were invited to London to become the first manager and chef of the Savoy Hotel, positions they held from 1889 until 1897. The Savoy under Ritz was an immediate success, attracting a distinguished and moneyed clientele, headed by the Prince of Wales. In 1897, Ritz and Escoffier were both dismissed from the Savoy, when Ritz was implicated in the disappearance of over 3400 Great Britain Pounds worth of wine and spirits. Before their dismissal, customers at the Savoy had reportedly urged them to open a hotel in Paris. Aided by a financier, Ritz purchased the palace and transformed the former Hôtel de Lazun building into a 210-room hotel. He stated that his purpose for the hotel was to provide his rich clientele with "all the refinement that a prince could desire in his own home." He engaged the architect Charles Mewès to update the original 1705 structure. Ritz's innovative standards of hygiene demanded a bathroom for every suite, the maximum possible amount of sunlight and the minimum of curtains and other hangings. At the same time, he furnished the hotel with all the old-fashioned appeal of an English or French aristocrat's home.

Grand Hotels: Reflections on Timeless Architectural Treasures

The hotel opened on 1 June 1898. Together with the culinary talents of his junior partner Escoffier, Ritz made the hotel synonymous with opulence, service, and fine dining, as embodied in the term "ritzy." It was among the first hotels in Europe to provide a bathroom en suite, a telephone and electricity for each room. It quickly established a reputation for luxury, with clients including royalty, politicians, writers, film stars and singers, but its sidewalk café and eclectic bars did attract a bevy of poor writers who flocked to Paris after World War I and became known as "the lost generation;" the most prominent, of course, being Hemingway and Fitzgerald. It immediately became fashionable with Parisian socialites, hosting many prestigious personalities over the years, such as Marcel Proust, F. Scott Fitzgerald, Ernest Hemingway, King Edward VII and the couturier, Coco Chanel, who made the Ritz her home for more than thirty years. Many of the suites in the hotel are named after famous patrons. Hemingway once said, "When in Paris the only reason not to stay at the Ritz is if you can't afford it." Hemingway, who stayed at the hotel many times after World War II, was there when he learned his wife wanted a divorce. He reacted to the news by throwing her photo into a Ritz toilet and then shooting the photo and the toilet with his pistol.

The building was extended in 1910, and César Ritz died in 1918, succeeded by his son, Charles Ritz. Queen Marie of Romania stayed at the Ritz Hotel with her two eldest daughters,

Grand Hotels: Reflections on Timeless Architectural Treasures

Elisabeth (of Greece) and Maria (of Yugoslavia) in 1919 while campaigning for Greater Romania at the Paris Peace Conference. Many other prominent royal figures and heads of state slept and dined at the hotel over the years. Edward VII reportedly once got stuck in a too-narrow bathtub with his lover at the hotel. August Escoffier died in 1935. In summer 1940, the Luftwaffe, the air forces of Nazi Germany during World War II, set up their headquarters at the Ritz, with their chief Hermann Göring.

After the death of Charles Ritz in 1976, the hotel went into a period of gradual decline. As it lost its former lustre, its clientele diminished, and for the first time in its existence it began to lose money. It was rescued, however, in 1979 by an Egyptian businessman, Mohamed Al-Fayed, who purchased the hotel for 20 million U.S. dollars. Al-Fayed renovated it completely over several years without stopping its operation; this was achieved by annexing two town houses, joined by an arcade with many of Paris's leading boutiques. The entire ten-year renovation cost a total of $400 million. The restaurants were given a new look, and a swimming pool, health club, and spas were created in the basement. One of the bars was renamed the Hemingway Bar. In 1988, the Ritz-Escoffier School of French Gastronomy was established in honour of Auguste Escoffier.

On 31 August 1997, Princess Diana and Al-Fayed's son Dodi, dined in the Imperial Suite of the hotel before leaving the hotel with bodyguard Trevor Rees-Jones, only to have a fatal car crash.

Grand Hotels: Reflections on Timeless Architectural Treasures

In the 21st century, the Ritz is ranked among the most luxurious hotels in the world and the most expensive in Paris. The hotel is home to L'Espadon, the world-renowned restaurant that attracts aspiring chefs from all over the world who come to learn at the adjacent Ritz-Escoffier School. The grandest suite of the hotel, called the Imperial, has been listed by the French government as a national monument in its own right. *(Imperial Suite)*

This is the room where Princess Diana had her final meal with Dodi Fayed. A journalist said after viewing the room, "The rich really know how to live, and royalty lives even better than the rich." The maid who accompanied him chimed in, "And the royals are smarter; they do it at taxpayers' expense."

Grand Hotels: Reflections on Timeless Architectural Treasures

This author asked the hotel if I could stay at the Ritz gratis, since I was writing a book that would include lavish praise for the hotel. Unfortunately, I was politely turned down. Still, I have not let that sway my assessment of the hotel.

L'Espadon Restaurant

Grand Hotels: Reflections on Timeless Architectural Treasures

Grandeur and the Ritz are synonymous!

11. Claridges's – Mayfair, London, United Kingdom

Claridge's was founded in 1812 as Mivart's Hotel, in a conventional London house, and grew by expanding into neighbouring houses. In 1854, the founder, George Mivart, sold the hotel to Mr. and Mrs. Claridge, who owned a smaller hotel next door. They combined the two operations, and after trading for a time as Mivart's at Claridge's, they settled on the current name. The reputation of the hotel soared when (now really take in this name) Doña María Eugenia Ignacia Augustina de Palafox y KirkPatrick, 16th Countess of Teba and 15th Marchioness of Ardales (5 May 1826 – 11 July 1920), known as Eugénie de Montijo (French), who was the last Empress Consort of the French Court from 1853 to 1871, and the wife of Napoleon III, Emperor of France, made an extended visit here and entertained Queen Victoria at the hotel.

Richard D'Oyly Carte, the theatrical impresario and founder of the rival Savoy Hotel, purchased Claridge's in 1894 to make it part of The Savoy Group, and shortly afterwards demolished the old buildings and replaced them with the present ones. This was prompted by the need to install modern facilities such as lifts and en suite bathrooms. The new Claridge's built by George Trollope & Sons, opened in 1898, and it has gone through many corporate owners over the years.

We ordinary mortals rarely can breath the same air as blue-bloods and here, along with kings, queens, princes, princesses and the fabulously wealthy, entertainers of renown have rested in sweet repose, including Cary Grant, Audrey Hepburn, Alfred Hitchcock, Brad Pitt, Joan Collins, Mick Jagger, U2 and Mariah Carey. Actor Spencer Tracy famously said, "When I die I don't want to go to heaven. I want to go to Claridge's."

Grand Hotels: Reflections on Timeless Architectural Treasures

Sometimes the blue-blood mentality can clash with the common nature of those of us who come from more humble circumstances and a controversy in 2014 caused a public relations disaster for Claridge's. A woman was breastfeeding her baby in the lobby, and the manager asked an employee to request that the lady cover herself with a shroud for the sake of discretion. Obviously, the manager was not aware of the UK's 2010 Equality Act, which made it unlawful for a business to discriminate against breastfeeding women. Three days later, several mothers staged a public breastfeeding protest outside Claridge's. Prime Minister David Cameron commented on the controversy, saying that he shared the view that breastfeeding is completely natural, and it was totally unacceptable for any woman to be made to feel uncomfortable when breastfeeding in public. For many days after the incident and the initial protest, there were demonstrations on the sidewalk in front of the hotel by mothers breastfeeding their children. Claridge's has never issued an apology for the incident, but for breastfeeding mothers, be absolutely assured that there will be no harassment by the staff or management of Claridge's if you breastfeed your child in the lobby, restaurant or anywhere else in the hotel. The adverse publicity did not hurt their business, but it did hurt their image.

Claridge's has become famed for its Christmas tree display as most years the tree is designed and decorated by someone notable in the fashion industry.

Grand Hotels: Reflections on Timeless Architectural Treasures

Christmas tree by Dolce-Gabbana

World War II's most famous 4-F (not draft-able) actor, John Wayne, frequented Claridge's when visiting or filming in London.

Grand Hotels: Reflections on Timeless Architectural Treasures

The feeling one gets when walking in is that you are entering a monument to aristocratic living that literally sparkles with opulence.

Grand Hotels: Reflections on Timeless Architectural Treasures

Open space emphasizes the grandeur of the hotel.

*A noted comic who once dined at Claridge's said,
"I only had my credit card, I did not realize that
I needed to bring the President of the Bank of England
in order to arrange a loan to pay my dinner bill."*

Lynton Globa Viñas

Grand Hotels: Reflections on Timeless Architectural Treasures

Yes, some rooms have grand pianos!

One guest said of Claridge's – "I expected the Queen to pop in any minute, sit down and ask me how things were going. I mean this place is nicer than Buckingham Palace."

12. The Shelbourne Hotel – Dublin, Ireland

O.K., we admit that the Shelbourne does not have an impressive exterior, but that old saying, "Never judge a book by its cover" is apropos here. It has a mystique to it, a certain sophistication, polished style and urbanity that exudes warmth and charm. It is not the place of the high-toned, the rich and the overly sophisticated. Rather, it is the embodiment of every man's right to be a part of the elite in a world where far too many of us seem to always be on the outside looking in. It is the epitome of an individual's right to be part of a world where each person is embraced and welcomed into the serenity of luxurious living.

Grand Hotels: Reflections on Timeless Architectural Treasures

The Shelbourne is a timeless landmark and a Dublin institution. It has been the scene of significant historical events, and is the iconic representation of sentimentality for a special way of life that is uniquely Irish. In May 1922, the hotel was the spot where Michael Collins and a few others drafted the Irish Constitution in room 112, now named the Constitution Room.

Perhaps, part of the hotel's charm is that it represents the quest for freedom by a people who felt oppressed by the rule of a foreign power. This is a different kind of luxury hotel. Years ago, author, J. Wayne Frye, referred to the hotel as "the equalitarian luxury hotel for those who dance in the sunlight of freedom expressed by the spirit of Michael Collins."

Grand Hotels: Reflections on Timeless Architectural Treasures

There are many quirks in regards to the hotel. For example, in the early 1900s, Alois Hitler, Jr., the elder half-brother of Adolf Hitler, worked in the hotel while living in Dublin. James Joyce is rumoured to have stayed in the hotel, and it is referenced in his most famous book, *Ulysses*.

The Shelbourne's stately brick facade, colonnaded entrance, intricate wrought iron fence, and doormen with top hats draw plenty of attention. In fact, it is not unusual for the flow of pedestrian traffic to slow or stop in front of the hotel as tourists pause to stare. The hotel makes an even grander impression once visitors pass through the wooden vestibule into the foyer, which has gleaming marble floors, crystal chandeliers, Palladian columns, gold gilding and intricate mouldings. The Lord Mayor's Lounge, an elegant space where afternoon tea is served, is a favourite of locals and the buzzing No. 27 Bar is one of the top places to see and be seen in the city. The Shelbourne has a long history of attracting notables that have picked this hotel. Famous guests have included Charlie Chaplin, Greta Garbo, Clark Gable, the Kennedys, Princess Grace, Julia Roberts, Charlize Theron, Liam Neeson, Bill Clinton and Bono.

To celebrate and commemorate its central role in the life of Dublin, the Shelbourne has a museum in the lobby of the hotel designed to showcase some of the fascinating memorabilia and items describing the engrossing history of this remarkable hotel, which is now part of the Marriot chain.

Grand Hotels: Reflections on Timeless Architectural Treasures

Although it has elegance and style, there is no stuffiness about this classic hotel. The top hats have been a tradition for over 100 years and although the rooms are a bit smaller than the other luxury hotels covered in this book, they have great charm and an ambiance that lifts the spirit.

Grand Hotels: Reflections on Timeless Architectural Treasures

There is a quiet elegance to the Shelbourne.

Grand Hotels: Reflections on Timeless Architectural Treasures

You enter through the oak doorways and bask in the subtlety of quiet opulence.

13. Chateau Monfort – Milan, Italy

You were promised a château in the introduction, and, although it is in the city, this was indeed, at one time, a grand chateau. The hotel building is an elegant historical structure, completed in 1903 and designed by Paolo Mezzanotte, who is also the acclaimed architect of the Italian stock exchange. The chateau was built for a family and each floor was assigned to one of the daughters, as a gift from their father. The building went through a harrowing 20th century and changed owners and purposes, until it was bought by an Italian family. The building became Château Monfort, as it is now called, after three years of extensive renovations (2009-2012) to reflect its storied history. Yes, it is a bit modern, but the history of the building makes it one of Europe's valued architectural treasures.

Grand Hotels: Reflections on Timeless Architectural Treasures

This is another one that a night time arrival is recommended for maximum aesthetic pleasure, and a piano player may be tickling the ivories when you walk into the lobby.

Grand Hotels: Reflections on Timeless Architectural Treasures

There is an interesting story about Château Monfrot. You see, it has a very special mascot, Juan Lapin, a playful bunny whose story is very much like a fairytale. Once upon a time, in an urban castle called Château Monfort, Ambrogio the magician lived with his beloved bunny Juan Lapin. Together they achieved great success, but one day Juan realized that even if fame made him happy, he lost one important thing: freedom. So he escaped from the château. Ambrogio desperately looked for him everywhere: in the Sala dell'Incantesimo, in the Alcova del Rubacuor, but there was no trace of Juan. So Ambrogio decided to continue his magic shows without his dearest friend. Then, one day, opening the doors of the Château, he saw many bunnies in front of the building, running around happy, and among them was his faithful friend Juan, glad to have found freedom and love, but Ambrogio captured him. Now, it seems that Juan Lapin and family are still imprisoned by the magician Ambrogio in the walls of Château Monfrot. Yes, there are strange noises in the walls at times, assumed to be descendents of Juan, or could it be Juan himself?

Grand Hotels: Reflections on Timeless Architectural Treasures

Luxury abounds in every suite.

All the sites of Milan are at your doorstep.

Grand Hotels: Reflections on Timeless Architectural Treasures

The name could hardly be more French, but the Chateau Monfort isn't the typical storybook chateau. To be fair, it isn't your typical Milanese hotel either. It begins with a classically French sensibility, but it's filtered through a postmodern imagination, and the result is about as far as you can get from the sober tones and high seriousness of Milanese luxury design. The public spaces are grand and the grandeur is not toned down in the rooms as the mixing of modern and classic elements titillate the senses.

Summary on Europe

An entire book could be written on European hotels alone. The space available simply does not allow for coverage of the hundreds of glittering monuments to the glory of a by-gone era. The ones selected are not necessarily the grandest of all, but rather are representative of the grandeur that can be found in the warmth of that which once scintillated and sizzled in an era when there were still skilled craftsman who took great pride in their work. The plastic, throw-away society we live in today rarely gives anything of real permanence. Today, utilitarianism is embraced to save money, streamline uniformity and increase the bottom line so the stockholders can reap maximum benefits. When most of the iconic structures covered here were built, it was about more than money. It was about how a hotel could represent art in its truest form.

Grand Hotels: Reflections on Timeless Architectural Treasures

CHAPTER 3
Mid-Asian Reflections in a Golden Eye

The exotic, pulsating vibrancy of Middle Asia mystifies and excites. Here are two magnificent hotels reflecting that image.

14. Taj Mahal Hotel – Mumbai, India

The Taj Mahal Palace Hotel is a Heritage Grand class five-star hotel located in Mumbai, Maharashtra, India, next to the Gateway of India. Historically it was known as the Taj Mahal Hotel or simply "the Taj."

It has 560 rooms, 44 suites and 1,500 staff. From a historical and architectural point of view, the two structures that make up the hotel are two distinct buildings, built at different times and in different architectural designs. The hotel's original building was commissioned by Jamsetji Tata and first opened its doors to guests in 1903. It is widely believed that Jamsetji Tata decided to

Grand Hotels: Reflections on Timeless Architectural Treasures

build the hotel after he was refused entry to one of the city's grand hotels of the time, Watson's Hotel, as it was restricted to whites only. Whether this is true or not is debatable.

Older structure to the left – newer to the right.
The hotel is probably best known now for the terrorist attack there in 2008 in which 167 people were killed.

Grand Hotels: Reflections on Timeless Architectural Treasures

Lynton Globa Viñas

15. Galle Face Hotel – Colombo, Sri Lanka

The Galle Face Hotel, opened in 1864, is one of the oldest hotels east of the Suez Canal. It is often referred to as one of the places everyone should see before they die. The hotel was originally built by four British entrepreneurs. Its name derives from the stretch of lawn which it faces, known as the Galle Face Green. The hotel was home to K.C. Kuttan, who began working there in 1942 as a bell boy and continued his employment until his death in 2014. Statistically, this is assumed to be the longest anyone was every employed by a hotel. Probably the most famous guest who ever bedded down here was Mahatma Ghandi.

Grand Hotels: Reflections on Timeless Architectural Treasures

Day or night, the grandeur is impressive.

Grand Hotels: Reflections on Timeless Architectural Treasures

CHAPTER 4

The Inscrutable East Asian Hotel Mystique

There is something intrinsically mysterious and exotic about eastern culture, and the hotels of the Far East are no exception. It is not just the design that is captivating, but the fascinating culture. Most of the hotels were built in the oppressive colonial era, when architects and builders had access to skilled artisans who were basically slave labour. Lack of justice in colonial times did not keep skilled artisans from doing the best work possible. Despite oppression, the pride they took in their work is reflected in every nook and granny of these magnificent structures that are a feast for the eyes. Like a grand banquet laid out with a cornucopia of delicacies, these hotels are true monuments to not just the visions of architects, but to the dedication of artisans who never wavered in devotion to their crafts.

16. Raffles - Singapore

Sometimes referred to as the crown jewel of Asian hotels, Raffles glistens and sparkles in the humid air like a cool ocean breeze that soothes the body in the heat of the day. It delights the eyes, but there is a serenity to it that soothes the soul as well. One feels a pleasurable ambiance that grips you with nostalgia for a simpler time when the world seemed less stressful.

Grand Hotels: Reflections on Timeless Architectural Treasures

Since 1887, Raffles has been an intoxicating blend of opulent luxury and impeccable service that offers an oasis from the hustle and bustle of the dynamic, spotlessly clean city of Singapore. (Yes, it is true that chewing gum is not allowed in Singapore – makes too much of a mess on the sidewalks.) There are 14 restaurants and bars in the hotel. Culinary delights are offered 24 hours a day for those with discerning palates. Although the food is presented like a Rembrandt painting with an array of colours and delightful placement of delicacies, probably the most awe-inspiring sight is the lobby that greets each guest with sweeping grandeur, seemingly unaltered from the turn of the century with huge white marble colonnades that encircle an atrium that soars three floors upwards.

This hotel pulsates with vibrancy.

Grand Hotels: Reflections on Timeless Architectural Treasures

During the Japanese occupation of Singapore (1942-1945), Raffles was renamed Syonan Ryokan, the Japanese name for occupied Singapore. Until the end of the war, Singapore, and with it the Raffles Hotel, remained occupied by the Japanese. It was reported that after the surrender of the Japanese forces in 1945, many Japanese officers and soldiers committed suicide in the hotel. Today, it is rumoured that some Japanese military ghosts have occasionally appeared, but fortunately, they are aware the war is over and are very peaceful.

17. Hotel Metropole – Hanoi, Vietnam

With American B-52 bombers buzzing overhead in 1971 and 1972, Jane Fonda and Joan Baez scurried from the Hotel Metropole to a nearby bomb shelter. Because foreign diplomats were know to stay in the hotel, the U.S. government avoided the

Grand Hotels: Reflections on Timeless Architectural Treasures

bombing of the Metropole, but the guests always went to the bomb shelter for fear that a mistake might be made. Dropping more bombs on North Vietnam than were dropped by all the allied powers in World War II, did not keep the USA from suffering a humiliating defeat, and the stories of the bombing raids are still told by old-time guests and employees at the hotel even today.

Yes, night time arrival is suggested here, too.

The Vietnamese are a people who never bend before tyranny, and their devotion to a cause is the stuff of legends. Their defeat of the most powerful country in the world is a reflection of their character and undying belief in freedom of the human spirit. This magnificent hotel is but a reflection of the Vietnamese character.

Grand Hotels: Reflections on Timeless Architectural Treasures

Vietnam is a nation that suffered through a terribly long war in search of its freedom from colonialism, so it is a bit ironic that a hotel from the colonial period stands boldly in a city that was nearly obliterated by the U.S. carpet bombing campaign.

18. Centara Grand Beach Resort - Hua Hin, Thailand
(Original Name: The Railway Hotel)

The hotel dates back to the time when Hua Hin was evolving into Thailand's first beach resort. The beauty of Hua Hin was noted by the engineers surveying the southern railway route in 1909. Land was set aside for a station, and in 1911 Hua Hin became a destination where wealthy Bangkok residents built their holiday homes.

Antonio Rigazai, the State Railways' Italian architect, designed the original building as a luxurious two-storey European-style resort hotel made of brick and wood, in accordance with royal command. The hotel opened in 1922. By 1928 the hotel's success led to expansion. After World War II, more guestrooms were added, along with restaurants, bars and a lobby with a panoramic view of Hua Hin Bay. In 1988, the hotel was purchased by Sofitel and became the Hotel Sofitel Central Hua Hin. Since 2014 it has been operated by CENTEL, Ltd. and was renamed the Centara Grand Beach Resort.

It is not immensely large but it is included here because of its Edwardian architecture that truly sets it apart from what one normally sees in the Southeast Asian resorts. A Chinese guest said of the Centara Grand: "It is not a hotel in the traditional sense. It lulls you into its arms with the welcoming smile of a mother offering comfort and love to a child. Here, you feel safe and loved."

Grand Hotels: Reflections on Timeless Architectural Treasures

Lynton Globa Viñas

19. The Manila Hotel – Manila, Philippines

For over 100 years, this hotel, often referred to as the *Grand Old Dame*, has stood majestic and proud at One Rizal Park in the heart of the city. The 570 room hotel is the oldest luxury hotel in the Philippines built in 1909 to rival Malacañang Palace, the official residence of the President of the Philippines and was opened on the commemoration of American Independence on July 4, 1912. Its penthouse served as the residence of General Douglas MacArthur during his tenure as the Military Advisor of the Philippines from 1935 to 1941. Atop the hotel complex, he lived in splendour and grandeur like royalty with his family, and many years later, when he scurried out of the country as the Japanese were taking Corregidor, while uttering his immortal, "I shall return" lament, no doubt, he was probably looking forward to another sojourn, upon his triumphant return, in the luxury of one of Asia's most iconic hotels.

Grand Hotels: Reflections on Timeless Architectural Treasures

The hotel contains the offices of several foreign news organizations, including *The New York Times*. It has hosted numerous world historical figures and celebrities including authors Ernest Hemingway and James A. Michener; actors Douglas Fairbanks, Jr. and John Wayne; publisher Henry Luce; entertainers Sammy Davis, Jr., Michael Jackson and The Beatles; U.S. President John F. Kennedy, British Prime Minister Anthony Eden, and other world leaders.

William E. Parsons, a New York City architect, hired to oversee construction, envisioned an impressive, comfortable hotel similar to a California mission, only much grander in scope. Later, this vision was refined when President Manuel Quezon hired Paris-trained Filipino architect Andrés Luna de San Pedro, son of a famous painter, to take charge of the renovations of the Manila Hotel in 1935. During the presidency of Ferdinand Marcos, the old Manila Hotel Company was liquidated and the government took over its ownership. The Government Service Insurance System (GSIS) was given the mandate to form a new subsidiary corporation that would restore, renovate, and expand the hotel. Mr. Marcos's wife, Imelda, could frequently be seen at the hotel restaurants. During her visits, a red carpet and garlands were put out and the air was sprayed with deodorant. Under Imelda's patronage, the hotel reaped international recognition and awards. It was the place to go and be seen during the Marcos years. After Marcos was deposed, as is common the world over,

Grand Hotels: Reflections on Timeless Architectural Treasures

it was decided to privatize the hotel. After a court battle, Chinese Filipino billionaire, Emilo Yap, took over the hotel. Today, it is one of the premiere hotels in Asia.

Grand Hotels: Reflections on Timeless Architectural Treasures

Grand Hotels: Reflections on Timeless Architectural Treasures

Lynton Globa Viñas

CHAPTER 5

South American Splendour

The Spanish Colonial style of architecture dominated in the early Spanish colonies of North and South America. It is sometimes marked by the contrast between the simple, solid construction demanded by the new environment and the Baroque ornamentation exported from Spain. The traza or layout was the pattern on which Spanish American cities were built in the colonial era. At the heart of Spanish colonial cities was a central plaza, with the main church, town council building, residences of the main civil and religious officials, and the residences of the most important citizens. The principal businesses were also located around this central plan. Radiated from the main square were streets at right angles and a grid that could extend as the settlement grew, impeded only by geography.

Grand Hotels: Reflections on Timeless Architectural Treasures

Hotels naturally reflected this style, and the first major hotels were built in the aforementioned centre of the traza. Unlike the mass suburbanization of North America, in the Southern Americas, central cities are the hubs of commerce and preferred for residences.

20. Plaza Hotel – Buenos Aires, Argentina

The Plaza was originally developed by local landowner and banker, Ernesto Tornquist. Facing San Martín Square, the nine-story hotel was lovingly designed by renowned German born architect, Alfred Zucker. It open in 1909, just a couple of months after Tornquist died.

Touted as the finest hotel in South America, it was also its most modern. The original hotel had central heating, telephone access and elevators. The hotel was wholly furnished by prestigious London decorators. Marble sculptures by the famed Gustav Eberlein of Germany and ceiling frescoes by Julio Vila Padres of

Grand Hotels: Reflections on Timeless Architectural Treasures

Spain added to the hotel's continental style. Its grandeur was hailed throughout South America, and it became a favourite haunt of exiled royalty from Europe. It also may have been used as a way-station by former Nazis passing through on their way to more friendly accommodations in the hinterlands to escape the war crimes trials in Nuremburg after World War II. The Marriot Corporation assumed management of the hotel in 1994, although it is still controlled by Tornquist's descendants.

21. Copacabana Palace – Rio de Janeiro, Brazil

The hotel is considered one of South America's premier hotels and has been in operation over 90 years. It faces the coast, and consists of an 8-story main building and a 14-story annex. The Art Deco hotel was designed by French architect Joseph Gire.

Many famous people have been guests at the grand Copacabana Palace, including the following: Madonna, Michael Jackson, Justin Bieber, Robin Williams, Elizabeth Taylor, Elton John, Walt Disney, the Rolling Stones, Rita Hayworth, Princess Diana, Marilyn Monroe and Luciano Pavarotti.

Facing the famous Copacabana Beach, this magnificent structure is in the heart of Rio. It vibrates and pulsates with action 24 hours a day, and has been the home of many wild tales. Orson

Grand Hotels: Reflections on Timeless Architectural Treasures

Welles threw furniture out of his room here in 1942. The filmmaker came to Rio to film a documentary and stayed for eight months at the Copacabana. Welles never finished the documentary, but when his girlfriend, Delores Del Rio, broke up with him he threw his furniture into the pool. This being Brazil, there was also lots of nakedness at the hotel. In 1939, Errol Flynn paraded down the hallways naked and Jayne Mansfield went topless by the pool in the 1960's. In Brazil, where bikinis are considered proper attire at nightclubs, this was pretty normal behaviour.

Grand Hotels: Reflections on Timeless Architectural Treasures

21. Hotel Patio Andaluz – Quito, Ecuador

Sometimes, a hotel is more than a facade. In this case, the hotel is actually two beautiful patios in a huge mansion. It has been around since the 1600's in one form or another and the quaintness of this place is soothing to the soul.

Grand Hotels: Reflections on Timeless Architectural Treasures

Here you can usually get a room for a reasonable price and a suite for only slightly more, just a block away from the Plaza Grande. It has a grand colonial ambiance that makes it feel like you are being transported to another time. The large courtyard, bright in the day, romantic at night, is occupied by an Ecuadorian International restaurant. The rooms are distributed over two levels of the two patios. This is a hotel with no pretensions, but it is a top notch contender for uniqueness.

Grand Hotels: Reflections on Timeless Architectural Treasures

There are no lifts, but the climb up the stairs is a delightful exercise into a glorious past when life was much simpler. This is not a place for those who crave the ostentatious. Rather, it is a journey into quite contemplative simplicity that makes one realize that there is a certain grandeur to the lack of adornments that accentuate fanciful, flamboyant, exhibitionistic pretentiousness.

CHAPTER 6
Grand Hotels in the Land of Guns, Flags and Patriotism

There is a land where old-time fundamentalism, guns, flag-waving and patriotism are as common as sand on a beach. It is a place where greed is promoted as an enviable trait, and everyone is taught that they can be fabulously rich. So, is it any wonder that grand edifices devoted to excessiveness and grandiose styles of living are available in abundance? There are so many luxurious hotels in this land of excess that it is difficult to pare down the list, but alas, we shall pick the top 5 in the United States.

22. Hotel Del Coronado – San Diego, California

Hotel Del Coronado sits serenely on San Diego's beachfront. It is the second largest wooden structure in the United States. When it opened in 1888, it was the largest resort hotel in the world. It

Grand Hotels: Reflections on Timeless Architectural Treasures

has hosted presidents, royalty and celebrities as well as being featured in numerous movies and books.

In November 1885, E. S. Babcock, retired railroad executive from Evansville, Indiana; Hampton L. Story, of the Story & Clark Piano Company of Chicago; Jacob Gruendike, president of the First National Bank of San Diego and Heber Ingle and Joseph Collett bought all Coronado and North Island, approximately 4,000 acres, for $110,000.

These men hired architect James W. Reid, a native of New Brunswick in Canada, who procured 2,000 labourers (Chinese) to create E.S. Babcock's visions for a grand hotel. Babcock's vision was specific: "It would be built around a court, a garden of tropical trees, shrubs and flowers. From the south end, the foyer should open to Glorietta Bay with verandas for rest and promenade. On the ocean corner, there should be a pavilion tower, and northward along the ocean, a colonnade, terraced in grass to the beach. The dining wing should project at an angle

Grand Hotels: Reflections on Timeless Architectural Treasures

from the southeast corner of the court and be almost detached to give full value to the view of the ocean, bay and city."

Getting all the lumber needed was a monumental problem, because it had to be imported from Northern California. The largest supplier of lumber in California, Dolbeer & Carson, brought in raw logs and set up an on-site saw mill. They cancelled all relationships with other builders to concentrate on this one project.

The Crown Room was Reid's masterpiece. Its wooden ceiling was installed with pegs and glue. Not a single nail was used.

When the hotel opened for business in February 1888, reports of the new grand hotel were wired across the country, but just as the hotel was nearing completion, Babcock and Story needed

Grand Hotels: Reflections on Timeless Architectural Treasures

additional funds and turned to sugar magnate, John D. Spreckels, who lent them $100,000 to finish the hotel. By 1890, Spreckels bought out both Babcock and Story. The Spreckels family retained ownership of the hotel until 1948, and a series of sales have followed over the years.

The popularity of the hotel was established before the 1920's. It already had hosted Presidents Harrison, McKinley, Taft and Wilson. Also, during this time, Hollywood stars were flocking to the hotel.

There are rumoured to be a few ghosts in the hotel, as several guests have died there over the years; some famous, some infamous and some neither. The words of author, Wayne Frye, after his first visit here in 1995, offer a cogent assessment of this magnificent edifice and how it motivates reflection on the state of life in the modern world. "Hotels that have been around for years have a mystique about them. Oh, and the ghosts that float about the corridors of captivating calmness seem to whisper the whimsical wishes of those who once knew life in a better time and better place. The Del Coronado is a hotel that pulsates with the ghosts of the past. It is not haunted by evil spirits, but by the dancing drama of a by-gone era; times when there were no televisions, no computers, no cell phones to clutter lives with the mundane mutterings of the merchants of commerce that tell us the good things in life can only be bought. There is no price tag on serenity, and this is a serene place plucked down on a small island near San Diego that requires only a stroll through its grounds to realize that this is not just an ordinary hotel – it is a time capsule of what has been lost in a nation that once embraced hope but now only knows the folly of rule by the oligarchy."

The grandeur of this hotel is spellbinding.

Barney Goodman purchased the hotel from the Spreckels in 1948. From the end of World War II until 1960, the hotel began to age until 1960, when local millionaire, John Alessio, purchased the hotel and spent $2 million on refurbishment and redecorating.

Mr. Alessio sold the hotel to Larry Lawrence in 1963, who invested $150 million to refurbish and expand it. He increased its capacity to 700 rooms. He added the Grande Hall Convention Center and two seven-story Ocean Towers just south of the hotel.

The Lawrence family sold the hotel to the Travellers Group after Lawrence's death in 1996 and it was sold many times over the intervening years, with the latest owners being Anbang Insurance Group, a Beijing-based Chinese insurance company, in a $6.5 billion hotel package deal. Perhaps it is fitting for the Chinese to own it after all these years. After all, while it was the vision of white businessmen, it was the immigrant Chinese labourers who actually did most of the hard work erecting this grand hotel.

23. Majestic Yosemite Hotel -Yosemite Park, California (Formerly the Ahwahnee Hotel)

Opened in 1927, this hotel at the base of towering mountains reflects the grandeur of the surroundings which titillate all the senses with its almost perfect setting among some of the most incredible scenery on the North American continent. The owners are technically the American people as the hotel is operated by concessionaires. The original named Ahwahnee Hotel was designed by noted architect, Gilbert Stanley Underwood. It is considered a masterpiece of rustic design, matching its surroundings. The site for the hotel is below the Royal Arches rock formation in a meadow area. The location was chosen for its views of iconic sights in Yosemite, including Glacier Point, Half Dome and Yosemite Falls.

The hotel is serenity at its finest, with the intense quiet sometimes seemingly almost overwhelming. Actress Judy Garland said, "There is a peace here that I can find no where else in the world. It is like the troubles you carry are somehow placed in a locked safe, and you hope the combination has been lost."

Grand Hotels: Reflections on Timeless Architectural Treasures

Grand Hotels: Reflections on Timeless Architectural Treasures

24. Waldorf Astoria Hotel – Manhattan, New York

There was a brief consideration to leave this one out, but alas, how can one write a book about grand hotels, and leave out what is probably the best known hotel in the world. Originally, the Waldorf Astoria had been housed in two historic landmark buildings in New York. The first, bearing the same name, was built in two stages, as the Waldorf Hotel and the Astor Hotel, which accounts for its dual name. That original site was situated on Astor family properties along Fifth Avenue, and opened in 1893. It was demolished in 1929 to make room for the Empire State Building. The present building, which is at 301 Park Avenue, is a 47-story 191 metre (625 Feet) Art Deco building completed in 1931. The current hotel was the world's tallest hotel until 1963, when it was surpassed by Moscow's Hotel Ukraina.

Conrad Hilton bought the hotel in 1972 and in 2014 it was sold to the aforementioned Abang Insurance Group of China for $1.95 billion U.S., making it the most expensive hotel ever sold. It has over 1400 rooms. Some of the suites have four bedrooms.

It is perhaps a bit ironic that the hotel is now owned by a Chinese company, as it was here, in this monument to capitalism's extreme excess, where many government officials met to rant and rave against communism in the early 1950's. This was during the Red Scare propaganda era that kept Americans in the throes of fear that the Red Hordes would swarm ashore and destroy the freedom of the capitalists to own more and more.

Grand Hotels: Reflections on Timeless Architectural Treasures

It was here, at the U.S. government's behest, that 48 prominent figures of the Hollywood film industry met to institute the infamous black list that banned anyone with communist beliefs or tendencies from working in motion pictures. This black list ruined many prominent writers, directors, producers and actors careers. So much for freedom of association and thought!

Listing all the celebrities and famous people who have stayed here would take up a large part of this book. Interestingly, many U.S. government officials stay here when in New York – at taxpayers' expense, of course.

Grand Hotels: Reflections on Timeless Architectural Treasures

Lynton Globa Viñas

Grand Hotels: Reflections on Timeless Architectural Treasures

25. Hotel Boulderado – Boulder, Colorado

The historic Hotel Boulderado opened in 1909 and the original Otis elevator is still in operation. The hotel's name comes from the words *Boulder* and *Colorado*. The hotel is listed on the National Register of Historic Places.

Rising majestically in downtown Boulder, surrounded by towering mountains, this historic hotel offers a respite from the modern, streamlined accommodations that lack character and soul. There is a serenity and calmness that accentuates the majesty of this extraordinary place.

26. Stanley Hotel – Estes Park, Colorado

Author Stephen King and his wife settled into Room 217 here for the night, and the rest, as they say is history – a history that was brought to the screen in the movie, "The Shining."

Grand Hotels: Reflections on Timeless Architectural Treasures

They were the only guests in the soon to close for the season hotel. He and his wife were served dinner in an empty dining room and then gleefully led down a long corridor to Room 217. That night, a dream struck King with inspiration for his next book. The hotel in King's book is an evil entity haunted by its many victims, and there have been a few reported ghostly sightings here, but none with any evil intentions. Of course, who knows what awaits down those lonely corridors? Want to see?

Freelan Stanley suffered from tuberculosis, and in 1903, he went to the mountains of Colorado for what he hope would be a cure. Apparently it was just what he needed, as he lived to be 91. So impressed with the fresh air and beauty of Colorado, he decide to make Estes Park into a tourist resort and began construction of a hotel which was completed in 1909. It was sold in 1930 and has gone though several owners since.

Grand Hotels: Reflections on Timeless Architectural Treasures

Grand Hotels: Reflections on Timeless Architectural Treasures

With the magnificent mountains as a backdrop, one would almost be willing to endure a few ghosts to enjoy the tranquil beauty of this extraordinary place.

27. Mark Hopkins Hotel – San Francisco, California

Author Wayne Frye said of this place: "I have written many books, but rarely does any of them generate the same enthusiasm as when I tell someone I am related to the Hopkins family, as my great grandmother was a Hopkins." Now, whether this was the same Hopkins for whom the hotel is named is debatable, as there were two Mark Hopkins who showed up in California at the same time. One was a businessman, and the other was a horse thief who had escaped from the noose in Randolph County, North Carolina. Again, a quote from Frye is apropos: "Frankly, I prefer to be a descendant of a rogue, rather than just a plain old boring millionaire businessman."

Grand Hotels: Reflections on Timeless Architectural Treasures

Although named the Mark Hopkins Hotel, he actually had nothing to do with building it. The hotel simply sits on a site where the Hopkins mansion once stood on Nob Hill, overlooking San Francisco. The mansion was destroyed by fire as a result of the 1906 earthquake, and the property was sold by Mark Hopkins' widow to mining engineer and hotel investor George D. Smith, who started construction on a hotel almost immediately.

The hotel stands tall and bold against the San Francisco skyline and looks down over the entire city, probably just as Mark Hopkins himself did at one time when he was one of the richest men in America.

Grand Hotels: Reflections on Timeless Architectural Treasures

The décor in the Mark Hopkins is referred to as refined opulence.

Grand Hotels: Reflections on Timeless Architectural Treasures

CHAPTER 7

Oh Canada – Hotels in the Mists of Time

Canadian, Rick Mercer once said, "I always believed there was a difference between conservative and stupid, but in the USA, it is getting harder to tell the difference." This, in a nutshell, sums up who Canadians are. Open-minded, embracing diversity, demanding that healthcare be a right rather than a privilege, insisting on a progressive tax structure that makes the rich pay a fair share and insisting on a firm separation of religion and state, these are a people who seem to dance to the beat of a different drummer in a world that wants obedience and conformity.

It is a nation that is consistently rated as one of the best places in the world to live, and the hotels reflect the diversity and magnanimity of a people who embrace real freedom, not the propagandized version that is so prevalent south of here.

Grand Hotels: Reflections on Timeless Architectural Treasures

The large number of iconic hotels that reflect the beauty of the people and the land could fill volumes rather than the few pages here, but the ones selected are representative of the glorious grandeur of a land that bristles with hope in a world that far too often grasps the mundane rather than the substantive.

The grand old hotels in Canada have a unique place in Canadian history. Many of them were built during the first quarter of the 20th century by the Canadian Pacific Railway, the Canadian National Railway or Grand Trunk Railway in order to provide elegant accommodations while their customers were travelling by train viewing the natural beauty along the rail line. The hotels were a natural adjunct to their passenger rail business. Later, the railroads sold them to international chains. These hotels are popular with tourists and locals alike and though overnight stays are expensive, they represent a fine piece of Canadiana worth visiting, even if you only have time for a walk through the lobbies. Two, Banff and Lake Louise, are major tourist resorts in their own right, located amid stunning Rocky Mountain scenery. However, we shall start on the east coast of Canada and work our way west.

28. The Westin Nova Scotian Hotel – Halifax, Nova Scotia

The Nova Scotian was built in 1928 by the Canadian National Railway. A company was hired to demolish the hotel, but it was saved when the property was purchased in 1996 by New Castle Hotels and Resorts. An additional $4 million was put into renovating the hotel and it reopened in 1997 as The Westin Nova Scotian.

The hotel as it appears today and in 1931.

Grand Hotels: Reflections on Timeless Architectural Treasures

29. The Château Frontenac – Quebec City, Quebec

The hotel is generally recognized as the most photographed hotel in the world, largely for its prominence in the skyline of Quebec City. The current hotel capacity is more than 600 rooms on 18 floors.

Grand Hotels: Reflections on Timeless Architectural Treasures

The Château Frontenac was designed by architect Bruce Price, as one of a series of château style hotels built for the Canadian Pacific Railway company during the late 19th and early 20th centuries; the newer portions of the hotel, including the central tower (1924), were designed by William Sutherland Maxwell. CPR's policy was to promote luxury tourism by appealing to wealthy travellers. The Château Frontenac opened in 1893.

Although several of Quebec City's buildings are taller, this landmark hotel is perched atop a tall cape overlooking the Saint Lawrence River, affording spectacular views.

Grand Hotels: Reflections on Timeless Architectural Treasures

Grand Hotels: Reflections on Timeless Architectural Treasures

33. The Chateau Laurier – Ottawa, Ontario

Fairmont Chateau Laurier, located near the intersection of Rideau Street and Sussex Drive, is designed in the French Gothic

Châteauesque style to complement the adjacent Parliament buildings. It is above the Rideau Canal locks and overlooks the Ottawa River.

The Château Laurier was commissioned by the president of the Grand Truck Railroad, Charles Melville Hays, and was

Grand Hotels: Reflections on Timeless Architectural Treasures

constructed between 1909 and 1912 at the same time as Ottawa's downtown Union Station. The hotel features original Tiffany stained-glass windows and hand-moulded plaster decorations dating back to 1912. There are conical turrets and dormer windows and the roof is copper. The gables are carved with flowers, scrolls and crests. The lobby floors were constructed of Belgian marble.

The hotel opened on 26 April 1912, but the head of the Grand Truck Railway that constructed it, Charles Melville Hays, who was returning to Canada for the hotel opening, perished aboard the *Titanic* when it sank on 15 April. A subdued ceremonial opening was held on 12 June 1912.

34. Royal York – Toronto, Ontario

Opened in 1929, the Royal York was built by the Canadian Pacific Railway across the street from Toronto Union Station. This was a time when railroads were king and knew almost no limits to their power.

Grand Hotels: Reflections on Timeless Architectural Treasures

35. Fort Garry Hotel – Winnipeg, Manitoba

Grand Hotels: Reflections on Timeless Architectural Treasures

As our train of architectural delight chugs along westward, the towering chateaus continue to impress. Built in 1913 by the Grand Trunk Pacific Railway, the Fort Garry Hotel is located one block from the railway's Union Station.

36. Bessborough Hotel – Saskatoon, Saskatchewan

The hotel was built by the Canadian National Railway from 1928 to 1932. The hotel was designed by Archibald and Schofield Architects of Montreal to resemble a Bavarian castle.

Grand Hotels: Reflections on Timeless Architectural Treasures

37. Banff Springs Hotel – Banff, Alberta

Nestling peacefully in one of the most picturesque settings of the grand and gloriously towering Canadian Rockies is the little town of Banff, a town that is lavishly endowed by nature with some of the most awe-inspiring scenery to be found upon the earth. In fact, the scenic environment of Banff is so colossal that it literally reduces the town itself to a mere speck, a tiny dot of civilization proudly courting Mother Nature in her grandest moods. The broad main street of Banff unrolls like a carpet to the base of Cascade Mountain, and there stops abruptly, as if powerless to penetrate the imposing barrier that blocks its way. In the middle of all this magnificence, glittering in glory is the mighty Banff Springs Hotel that sparkles like a freshly polished diamond.

Grand Hotels: Reflections on Timeless Architectural Treasures

Views from the room balconies are so over powering it almost takes one's breath away,

Built by the Canadian Pacific Railroad, the original hotel opened in 1888 and was replaced by the current structure in 1911. There are few places that can assault the senses the way Banff does. Along with nearby Lake Louise, Banff is probably one of the most incredible monuments to the utter power of nature to assault all our senses and make us realize just how insignificant we all are in the grand scheme of things. This is a magical place that embraces all who gaze upon it with the majesty of nature.

Grand Hotels: Reflections on Timeless Architectural Treasures

Grand Hotels: Reflections on Timeless Architectural Treasures

A journey across Canada can still be enjoyed by train from east to west as the grandeur of this wonderful land is laid before you in all its glorious splendour. Yes, it is more expensive than flying, but the rewards are worth the extra expense. The Canadian government, eschewing the privatization mania that swept across the USA with the introduction of Reagan's culture of greed wilfully subsidizes rail travel for the benefit of all. When one chugs along through the Canadian Rockies and approaches the magnificence of Banff, it is little wonder that you understand what author, Wayne Frye, said of Canada: "This is a land that moves inexorably forward, but it never loses sight of the things that make life truly rewarding."

38. Fairmont Lake Louise Chateau – Lake Louise, Alberta

Only a short 60 kilometres from Banff is yet another grand monument of elegance and charm that creates awe in all lucky enough to gaze upon the glorious grandeur of a truly unique edifice that has seemingly been plucked down into what one might well visualize as heaven on earth. The original hotel was gradually developed at the turn of the 20th century by Canadian Pacific Railways and resembles its predecessors, the Banff Springs Hotel and the Château Frontenac.

Grand Hotels: Reflections on Timeless Architectural Treasures

Waking up to this view is intoxicating.

Lynton Globa Viñas

Grand Hotels: Reflections on Timeless Architectural Treasures

39. Hotel Vancouver – Vancouver, British Columbia

The journey by rail concludes in beautiful Vancouver. There were two previous Hotel Vancouver's, but the last incarnation opened in 1939 and has been a landmark in the city ever since. Built by the Canadian Pacific Railway, it is affectionately called the *"Castle of the City."* Today, it is, along with the Empress Hotel in Victoria, British Columbia, one of the most iconic hotels in North America.

Grand Hotels: Reflections on Timeless Architectural Treasures

40. Empress Hotel – Victoria, British Columbia

Grand Hotels: Reflections on Timeless Architectural Treasures

Vancouver Island is separated from the city of Vancouver by the Georgia Strait, and the capital of British Columbia is not Vancouver, but Victoria, which is on Vancouver Island. This incredibly beautiful place was the perfect spot for the Edwardian, château-style hotel, which was designed by Francis Rattenbury for Canadian Pacific Railways as a terminus hotel for Canadian Pacific's steamship line, whose main terminal was just a block away. The hotel was to serve businesspeople and visitors to Victoria, but later as Canadian Pacific ceased its passenger steamship services to the city, the hotel was successfully remarketed as a resort to tourists. The hotel was built between 1904 and 1908. Additional wings were added between 1909 and 1914, and in 1928. During this time, the Empress played hostess to kings, queens, movie stars and many famous people. In the 1930s, famous child star Shirley Temple arrived, accompanied by her parents, amid rumours that she had fled from California because of kidnapping threats.

In 1999, Canadian Pacific spun off Canadian Pacific Hotels, along with all its properties. It has gone through several owners since, but the ambiance and charm of this extraordinary place has remained in tact.

Strolling through the hotel is like a magical trip back into time. The attention to detail makes one appreciative of the efforts by superior craftsmen to create a lasting impression in this architectural marvel.

Grand Hotels: Reflections on Timeless Architectural Treasures

Victoria is a city that delights in its grandeur and embraces the mantra "there are no strangers, only new friends to be made."

Grand Hotels: Reflections on Timeless Architectural Treasures

Strolling leisurely though the hotel, there is a feeling of reverence that abounds, almost as if the hotel is alive with history pulsating all about.

Grand Hotels: Reflections on Timeless Architectural Treasures

The hotel is well known for its classic Victorian afternoon tea service. The hotel serves tea (along with sandwiches, fresh scones, preserves and clotted cream) in its Tea Room to more than 800 guests daily. Advance reservations are a must, as is a hefty bank account.

EPILOGUE
A Vision into Reality

It is said that beauty is in the eye of the beholder. So, not all the hotels here will catch the eye of every reader. The real nature of beauty is often more esoteric than physical. A great architect once said: "No building will stand forever, but if it has a solid foundation, it may indeed endure for thousands of years."

Unfortunately, we live in a world today where foundations are far too shallow. Ours is a throw away society in a throw away age. Instead of honouring and preserving the past, it is torn down, ingloriously shoved aside, laughed at with utter disdain and unceremoniously dismissed as irrelevant. Far too many grand and glorious structures have been obliterated by the wrecking balls of greed, which bases every decision on the bottom line of a balance sheet.

Grand Hotels: Reflections on Timeless Architectural Treasures

In a world where greed is promoted as an enviable trait that fuels ambition, we need to cling to some of the grandeur of the past. The past must not be overly glorified, because far too many people long for a past where things were not a good as they think they were. Yet, artistically speaking, one can look at structures that have stood the test of time and these grand edifices still inspire awe after all these years.

In the final analysis, grand hotels are more than just buildings. They speak to the human spirit. They are poetry in brick, mortar and wood. They are paintings on the canvas of grandeur. They are the sculptures of artists who shaped a vision into reality.

The End
Don't Miss *Haunted Hotels: Transitory Dances with the Dead* by Lynton Viñas

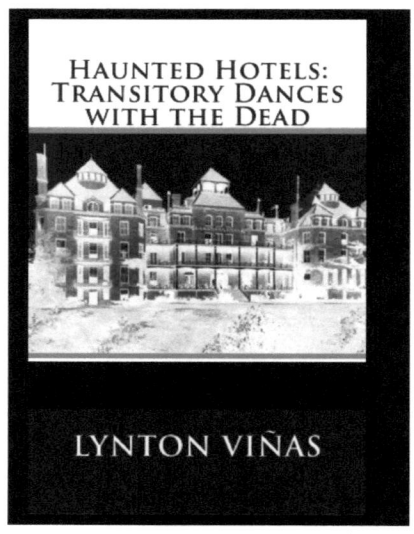

www.ingramcontent.com/pod-product-compliance
Lightning Source LLC
Chambersburg PA
CBHW041611220426
43669CB00001B/6